PRACTICE
MADE
PERFECT

How anyone can master anything quicker, easier and better than ever.

Roberto Moretti

Dedicated to the vision of a more talented humanity.

About the Author

Self-confessed as someone "Cursed with far too little talent and far too much persistence, " Roberto Moretti (pictured on front cover) dedicated himself first-hand to perfecting the art of practice.

His journey led him to explore the teaching and learning of a variety of different skills, each of which helped illuminate different ideas and concepts that would aid in developing a universal method for better acquiring skill.

His goal was never necessarily mastery, but rather being able to easily maintain consistently rapid progress in any skill, regardless of the initial level of his natural talent (which was often non-existent).

Practice Made Perfect is the summation of thousands of hours of real-world practice, observation and experimentation, all distilled down into an incredibly simple, yet ridiculously effective guide to perfect practice and serious results.

For the latest from Roberto, please visit
www.robertomoretti.com

Table of Contents

Preface

I'll be the first to agree that to come up with a system that shows how 'anyone can master anything quicker, easier and better' is an ambitious task; in fact find it hard myself to believe that I'm the one who has ended up writing this.

My vision was to create a practical 'how-to' book written from real-world experience, for real-world application which would lead to serious tangible results. It is for this reason that I've tried to keep it as short and succinct as possible and have done away with anything that I thought was unnecessary or impractical.

The real challenge and work in writing this book was being able to unify and simplify all the knowledge that was out there and all that I discovered firsthand into a straightforward system that anyone can use, and I hope it lives up to that vision.

Practice Made Perfect

Taking the time to acquire and read something like this shows that you are truly dedicated and devoted to excelling in your chosen skill, and for that you have my deepest respect.

I sincerely hope what follows lives up to your expectations and takes you to all new levels of mastery and better learning, but most of all puts an end to any doubts, frustrations and lack of progress you may be experiencing in the development of your own talent, in whatever field it may be.

When all is said and done, the human mind is a thing of infinite complexity; this is but one man's humble attempt at providing a way of using it better.

Roberto Moretti

Introduction

Practice Makes Perfect. For a phrase that consists of only three words, it opens worlds of possibility.

Absolutely any time we learn to do something, if we want to be able to do it well, we need to practice. Some things can be learnt in minutes, while others can take a lifetime, but regardless, practice is still an inescapable fact of life.

For something that is so universal and necessary, it truly makes you wonder, why haven't people learnt to do this crucial activity as best they can?

Often so much emphasis is placed on **what** is being learnt, that we tend to ignore the great benefits that could to be gained by improving **how** we actually go about learning.

This book will guide you in mastering the art and science of practice so you will in effect become 'talented at becoming talented.'

We all possess an unlimited potential for acquiring talent and skill and the way to do so will be mapped out so you can and will do it in a way that is, as it says on the front cover, 'quicker, easier and better than ever.'

I would like you to imagine for just a moment...

What if you were a person who could get good quickly at absolutely anything? What if you knew you could acquire any skill up to any level? What if you could become talented at becoming talented?

Would things be different?

This is about to become a reality, because the secret to possessing great talent lies in mastering the art of practice.

I want you to get better at your chosen skill and reach your goals as soon as possible, as easily as possible and even take you further in your mastery than you even thought was possible.

What follows is more than just a few handy hints on improving your practice; it is a **complete system and method** for better learning developed through years of trial and error in many different skills.

It's beneficial to note that this isn't necessarily a book about how to learn, it is a book about how to learn **more efficiently.**

The truth is that you have likely effectively learnt to do a great variety of things in your lifetime, so you must have been doing something right!

It isn't a coincidence that people who consistently get better with practice find they already know or do some things mentioned in this book, and in fact any time you have ever learnt to do anything through practice and achieved results, you have likely also applied some of what follows.

However, you are now making yourself conscious of the learning process and optimising it for *maximum results*. You are now making yourself conscious of what you have been doing which will allow you to consciously improve how you go about it.

While this is a complete guide to the art of practice and skill acquisition, this book is here more to 'help you fill in the pieces' than anything else, to find what is lacking in your approach to practice so you can take it to the next level.

Practice Made Perfect

This book may be concise, but it packs quite a punch. By the time you finish it, you will join the few that know pretty much all there is to know when it comes to developing their unlimited potential talent as best they can.

If you can find as little as one new idea in this entire book that you apply, the effort in reading would have been worth it.

So without further ado, let's begin...

Part 1: The Nature of Learning and Skill

The first part of this book is here to teach you the background information about the nature of skills and the process of how to go about learning them. This is important because we can't optimise the way we learn without first understanding what it entails.

You see, there may be an almost infinite number of skills out there, but they all share element in common, they all have to be learnt using the same machinery, the human mind.

The intricacies of the billions of possible skill are all different (that is, the 'content' that we have to learn and practice) however, we all share the same learning mechanism, our brains. Regardless of your chosen skill, the way your brain learns (the context) is universal.

The content of what you learn, your chosen skill, is up to you, but when it comes to installing it into your mind, the context will always be the same, and it's time to become aware of **exactly** what that is.

By understanding how skills are made up, how our brains are designed to work and the process by which we learn, we can go on to change the way we practice to better suit these things. Knowledge is power.

The Learning Machine

The machinery that we as humans possess that ultimately allows us to learn and acquire any skill is our physical brains and our conscious focus (our mind).

Thousands of pages could have been written about these two fascinating things, but what we really need to worry about are two key concepts that underlie all learning.

We don't need to worry about the finer academic concepts of neuroscience because all we are doing is training in interrelated actions and responses, almost in a machine like way so all the benefits we need lie in understanding what relates to that.

These concepts aren't very complex, but they are the backbone to learning any skill...

KEY CONCEPT 1

"Anything done consistently and continuously will eventually become habitual."

Have you ever noticed that after you have done

something several times, it begins to take less effort to do?

This is because your mind habituates repeated actions, and in turn makes them automatic and effortless. That is, they begin to occur unconsciously and without us needing to focus and concentrate on doing them so much, even to the point where we hardly need any focus at all.

For those interested in the science behind this, the explanation is very simple. When you repeat something enough, your brain strengthens the pathways between electrical transmitters (called neurons) in the brain and body that cause this sequence of actions.

When you are practicing, you are consciously causing neurons to fire one after another to cause you to act in a way to achieve a desired outcome, but as these sequences are repeatedly fired through your own conscious volition, your nervous system begins to strengthen these pathways for easier and rapid retrieval later. As these pathways become strengthened through practice, the need for conscious focus deteriorates as the brain fires the neurons in proper sequence habitually.

Practice Made Perfect

This phenomenon is often termed 'muscle memory', but the truth is that it's not your muscles that remember, but rather your nervous system as a whole, with your brain playing the key central role.

This simple tendency (for actions to become habitual through repetition), is the cornerstone of learning any skill. Any skill is nothing more than a collection of automated responses and actions, which have been literally engrained into your brain.

When we are learning a skill, we are just building and strengthening neural pathways. If we can master the art of building neural pathways, we have mastered the art of learning any skill.

The key to this lies in the words 'consistently and continuously'. By 'consistently and continuously' doing the correct actions that make up your skill, you form the backbone of effective practice. We will look into this in much more detail a little later.

For now, we need to consider that as far as these neural pathways are concerned, we can only build so many of them at any one time, which leads us to our next key point...

KEY CONCEPT 2

"Your brain has an unlimited capacity, but a limited focus."

It's strange to think, but as humans we really don't actually have a limit to the amount of skills or depth of skill that we can learn.

Think about it, imagine if you went to learn something new, only to find out that you were out of space and couldn't learn anything ever again, or the even more humorous situation of 'every time I learn something new, I forget to do something I've learnt in the past'. Luckily, this is not the case.

When it comes to the amount of possible neural connections that our brains can form, scientific research has shown that the storage capacity is so immense it's almost inconceivable. It's not that we even have a fixed set of connections; rather we have the **ability to grow more!**

Some excellent examples of this include a study where MRI tests showed in musicians that played stringed instruments that the area of brain controlling finger movements had actually grown. [1]

This ability for the brain to grow has been termed **Neuroplasticity** and it has become a revolutionary discovery and key area of interest for scientists in recent years. While it is a complex field of neuroscience, the upshot is that what it means for us is simply that the capacity of our minds is not only enormous, it may well be unlimited!

Make no mistake, this characteristic is nothing short of phenomenal, it pretty much means that you have **no limits.** The weakness of our potential for learning lies not in its capacity, but rather in the limited rate in which we are able learn and fill it.

You see, when it comes to doing any learnt behaviour, there are always two forces at play at any one time. The first is what happens unconsciously (that is, without us thinking, things that are well learnt and thus already 'automatic' and 'habitual') and the second is what we are thinking about and focusing on consciously.

So what is the problem? Well, we have the capacity to learn **so much** (unconscious capacity) as a whole, but at any one time we have such an extremely limited amount of focus that we can use to learn and build new neural pathways. Not only that, often people don't even know how to use this limited focus properly to improve and don't go anywhere, and through improper practice can even go backwards.

At any one time your level of skill is what you have trained in (the unlimited unconscious component) and what you can direct your limited focus towards (the heavily-limited conscious component).

Let's express this visually...

Figure 1: Unconscious and Conscious Skill

In the diagram above, the dark grey area represents the part of your skill that you are doing or have trained in to do to the point where it is unconscious

Practice Made Perfect

(no longer requires your focus), whereas the light grey part represents the extra skill you can have by utilising your available conscious focus. Think of practice as using your focus repeatedly to 'colour in' the light grey area so it becomes unconscious and allows you to then focus on something else (making the bar longer, and increasing your overall skill).

Your unconscious mind can process billions of bits of information per second, yet the conscious mind's focus is limited to the hundreds.

The irony is that in order for something to become unconscious and stored in the limitless capacity that is our brain, we must first put it in there using our highly limited conscious focus, piece by piece.

To do this, you need to know specifically what skills are and how they are built, which will be the focus of the next part.

1.   T.Elbert, C. Pantev, C.Wienbruch, B.Rockstroh & E.Taub "Increased Cortical Representation of the **Fingers of the Left Hand in String** Players", Science 270, 5234 (1995): 305-307

Skill

What is Skill?

Now that you understand how the mind works, it's time to move on and develop an understanding of the nature of how skills work. What is a skill? At its most basic level, the best way to define a skill is as anything that you can **learn to do**.

In fact, absolutely anything that anyone is capable of doing can be considered a skill-set.

> ***Skill-Set***: *a set of interrelated actions and/or responses that serve to produce a common outcome or related collection of outcomes.*

Even seemingly mundane and common everyday activities such as cleaning, ironing and driving are in fact skill-sets. In fact, some skills aren't even physical in nature; consider something such as being persuasive or a good public speaker, these things can also be considered skill-sets.

Learning a skill is simply a matter of turning things that you can't do, into things that you can do. That is, **constantly turning inabilities into abilities.** It is very rare for a whole skill to be just one action, as mentioned in the definition above they are usually sets of interrelated actions. The individual actions within each set can also further be broken down into their components. Skills all tend to follow this **hierarchical structure.**

Generally what this means is that in all skills, there are very general and wide-encompassing abilities at the top, and more specific ones towards the bottom, that make up the ones on the higher levels.

For example let's take a straight punch from Karate and see where it lies on the hierarchy...

Practice Made Perfect

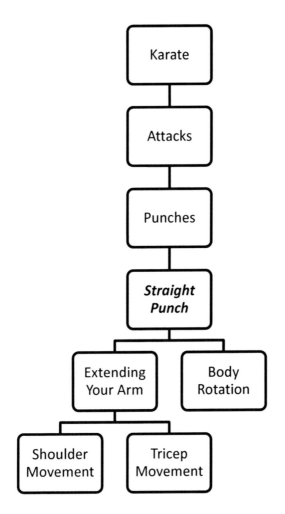

Figure 2: An Example Skill Hierarchy

Notice how being able to extend your arm and rotate your body are what lead to being able to do a straight punch, and simultaneously you being able to do a straight punch itself is one of the components of you being able to do punches in general?

Parts of a Skill (what I call 'modules') are all a matter of being able to do something (an ability), and a number of these modules get put together to form parts of a higher **level of abstraction.**

As you go up in the diagram you are at a higher level of abstraction, and each box represents a **module.**

> **Module:** A part of a skill that you are focusing on at any one time.

All skills are built this way. The higher level the module, the more data there is inside it, because it includes all the data in lower level modules that make it up **plus** the data it takes to join them together into one module (or 'chunk', which is another term for this that some people tend to use).

Of course, each module represents its own ability in and of itself and can be classed as a skill in its own right (for example, rotating your body can be considered a skill in itself.)

Because each module is made up by more than one module underneath it, with every lower level there are more modules, and so the hierarchy of modules in any skill tends to form a **pyramid-like structure.** As you go down to lower levels of abstraction, the more modules there are.

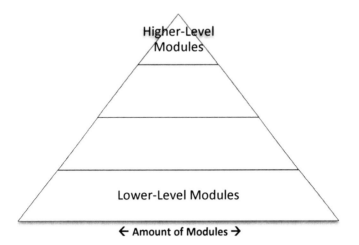

Figure 3: The Pyramid-Like Structure of Skill Hierarchies

Of course, if you were to draw every imaginable part of your skill-set, you would have a chart that not only would be enormous, but chances are that many modules would be interrelated with other ones all over the place.

Drawing a chart of your chosen skill's hierarchy is not necessary, but what you do need to understand is that each module is made up of lower level modules and forms part of a higher level module.

Anytime you are focusing on practicing something you can either...

    a. **Chunk Up** (go to a higher level) by asking 'what does this module form a part of?' or 'what is this module an example of?' and then focusing on that.

    b. **Chunk Down** (go to a lower level) by asking 'what are the individual components of this?' or 'what is an example of this?' and then choosing one of those to focus on.

Remember, the conscious mind can only focus on a tiny bit of data at one time, so if you don't have lower level modules deeply engrained in your brain, you will experience great trouble learning higher level ones, because to learn a higher level module by itself is just too much data for you to focus on at one time. Think of the lower level modules as being the foundation building blocks of the building that is your skill. You cannot add another storey if the foundation is not strong enough.

Breaking down a skill to a level you can focus on and practice with a high degree of perfection is a key process in perfect practice, and this will be discussed more in the chapter on **Isolation.**

Now that we understand the way in which the mind learns, and how skills can be arranged and broken up, let's take a look at the process of learning and the stages of competency we experience as we learn and practice each individual module...

The Learning Process

The Three Parts

When learning any skill, there are three key parts to the skill acquisition process.

These are resources, focus and our neurology (your brain and nervous system).

Content   **Context**

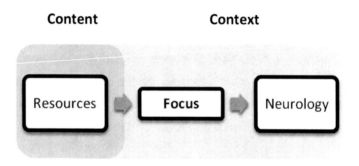

Figure 4: The Skill-Set Acquisition Process

1. Resources

Resources are the sources of 'know-how'. Examples include books, teachers, videos and other sources of instructional knowledge.

We are lucky in that we live in a world where

information is so readily accessible. The resources available out there are near-unlimited and are invaluable in providing us with the explanations and demonstrations of what we need to practice.

2. Focus (Mind)

This is our conscious focus that we use to create new neural pathways. It is limited in that we can only access so much of it at any one time. As a result of this, it is very much a bottleneck which data must pass through between the unlimited resources out there and the unlimited capacity as we learn.

3. Neurology (Brain)

This is our unlimited storehouse and memory for unconscious ability.

It is unlimited in two ways, the first is in capacity and storage (no limits to learning) and the second is in activity (the unconscious mind can process billions of bits of data per second in real-time).

In summary, resources tell us what to practice, focus is the consciousness that does the practice itself, and neurology is what is stored in our brain as a result of practice.

The 'Resource Trap'

Have you ever found that you have, or have known someone who has done a lot of reading about a particular skill, knows seemingly everything about it, yet when it comes to actually doing it they are completely unable to?

That is, they have the knowledge, but they don't have skill (knowledge comes from reading how or watching a demonstration, actual skill comes from practice).

This is what I call the **resource trap**, knowing too much but doing too little.

Almost all books tend to give people an understanding, but what's important is that it leads to tangible action that produces results.

Rather than just understanding perfect practice, we want it to become a tangible reality for you.

With this book non-fiction and instructional, its goal isn't necessarily to entertain you, but rather to help you achieve solid, tangible results.

So be sure to apply what's in this book whenever and wherever possible.

Stages of Competency

In the learning and practice of any module, there are four key 'stages of competency' that you will move through.

Figure 5: The Four Progressive Stages of Competency

These stages are actually a widely-accepted model of learning that has been around for quite a while and isn't credited to anyone in particular.

I am introducing you to these four stages because in the second part of this book we are going to go one step further by showing you specifically what takes you from stage to stage and how to do it most efficiently.

The four stages are,

1. Unconscious Incompetency

This is the first phase of learning. It is marked as

either an inability to do the skill or module in question (that is, you can't do it) and either...

a. Ignorance (you just don't know how to do it) or
b. Delusion (you think you can do it, but actually aren't producing the desired outcome)

The way to progress from this stage is by developing an awareness of both what it is you are unable to do and of what the perfect execution of a module actually entails. This is achieved through consulting your resources and is the process I call **Identification**.

2. Conscious Incompetency

This is where you find your way out of your ignorance or your delusion, and awareness emerges as you realise not only what you are incapable of doing, but why. That is, you are now aware of the correct way of doing it.

However, despite knowing why, you still may not be able to actually do it. The way out of this stage is by becoming actually able to perform the module (or parts of it) properly, and this can only be achieved by reducing the amount of data you are focusing on to an amount small enough for you to be able to execute with a high amount of perfection. That is, reducing the data load to an amount that your limited conscious focus can reasonably handle. This process is called **Isolation**.

3. Conscious Competency

This stage is characterised by your ability to do a part of your skill-set as a result of consciously focusing on it.

While you technically can do what you need this way, you still want to make it unconscious because you need to free up your conscious mind to learn more. You free up your conscious resources by making the module unconscious through the process called **reinforcement**, which is essentially a large degree of properly executed repetition.

4. Unconscious Competency

This is the final stage where a skill or part of a skill becomes habitual and automatic. This is the stage where a person, assuming that you are doing everything right, has mastered a part of or the skill as a whole.

It's strange to think that it is no more effort for a master to perform a skill's hardest techniques than it is for a beginner to do the more simple ones, because a master has trained it in unconsciously so it is automatic.

Once we achieve this level and really have laid the strong neural pathways in our mind that we need to, it leaves the limited focus of the conscious mind open to learn the next level or a new part of a skill (**Escalation**) and we improve and our talent increases.

If enough lower level modules have been learnt unconsciously, this then gives the opportunity to practice them all together in order to join them into a higher level module. This process is known as **Integration**.

It is a very cyclical process, because there are infinite ways you can improve on a skill, and every time you learn something, it creates something else that you can't do. It's up to you to decide what you will learn next depending on your goals.

What Does It _Really_ Take to Get Good?

Let's imagine a period of time, it could be any length of time, but for argument's sake let's make it three months. In those three months, the improvement you make in your chosen skill can be anything from zero (absolutely no improvement) to a very large improvement.

How much you will improve within that time can be simplified down into two key categories, both of which you can and will soon learn to control.

These two categories are the **quality** and the **quantity** of your practice.

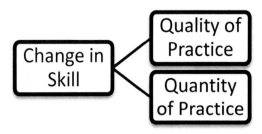

Quality of Practice

Quality of practice is essentially how well you are practicing. That is, the rate at which the practice that you are doing actually produces tangible results.

Quantity of Practice

Quantity of Practice is simply the total amount of time that you have practiced.

Increase these two things and you will increase your level of skill in a given period, it really couldn't be simpler.

All we need to do is increase both of these factors as much as we can and the result is more skill in less time! We will be going in depth into what we can do to increase both.

A lot of people tend to think the longer you've been doing a skill, automatically the better you will be. While it is true to an extent, it's not the amount of years you've been doing a skill that counts, it's the quantity and quality of practice that you have put into them.

What About 'Natural Talent'?

In general, people like to think if you don't have natural talent from the get go that you are doomed to fail and there is nothing you can do about it.

Natural talent can be very beneficial, and if you are one of the lucky few that possesses it, all the best to you, but unfortunately **no matter how much natural talent you have initially, there comes a point where everybody learns at the same rate.**

Remember how when we build a skill we are just laying neural connections in our mind? Well natural talent is a person's inclination to have strong pre-existing neural connections in their mind for lower level modules that link up and allow them to learn a skill with relative ease.

How did these connections get there? Sometimes it is genetics, but it could also be because they built neural connections from learning other things that are useful in transferring over to this new skill with a little practice.

If you have natural talent for your chosen skill, that's great and you are certainly lucky, but if you don't then that it is still okay, because we all have the exact same limited focus and unlimited capacity to learn.

Practice Made Perfect

You need to realise that your potential is not determined by the level of your natural talent, but rather by what you choose to learn and the way you go about installing it into your brain. In the long run, quality and quantity of practice will always win out over the short term advantage that natural talent may provide, so don't be discouraged.

Neurologically speaking, we are all using the same machinery to learn and act, and if one person is able to do something, another person can achieve the same results as long as they can deconstruct it and know the proper way to practice.

If you are being taught something or are trying to practice something that you just can't do, it just means you are focusing on too high a level module, and need to perfect lower level modules first.

So, if you think you 'can't do' something, it's not true, it is just that you can't do it at the moment, anyone can do anything if they know how to install it properly through practice.

It's true, the idea of infinite potential does seem a little up in the clouds, but given the idea of neuro-plasticity we've come to see that the capabilities of our brain, even if they aren't infinite, are certainly more than we could ever utilise.

There is one limitation however, and that lies in the physical. At the end of the day the brain may be able to learn any number of responses, movements, actions and solutions, but genetically our muscles have a limited potential for speed and strength in executing them that can only be developed to a certain point.

That said, perfect practice still breeds perfect technique, and with that you will likely be quite surprised at how far seemingly inferior genetics can and will take you.

Part 2: The 'Practice Made Perfect' System

Now that we have covered the systems of learning and understand how they work, the next step is to take what we know and use this knowledge to benefit ourselves.

Recall the two key concepts, **everything comes from them...**

1. **Any pattern of action done** <u>**consistently**</u> **and** <u>**continuously**</u> **eventually becomes habitual.**

2. **Your brain has an unlimited unconscious capacity, but a limited conscious focus.**

Practice Made Perfect

Practice does not necessarily make perfect, practice will only make habitual. Perfect practice is what makes perfect.

Of course it would be impractical and a gigantic process to tell you the nuances of practicing every single skill, but these are five certain processes that constantly need to be going on during your practice, five processes that if followed, will drastically increase your quality of practice, and in turn your results and growth in talent.

These processes are simple, yet enormously powerful. As I mentioned earlier everyone already has a model of how to practice, but it is largely unconscious and often you won't realise how you even go about it until it is pointed out to you.

Keep in mind that the following processes are happening all the time, on both higher and lower levels of abstraction, as discussed earlier.

In a nutshell, the five processes comprise of...

Practice Made Perfect

1. **Identification** – Becoming aware of the module that you are going to practice and exactly what being able to do it perfectly entails.

2. **Isolation** – Choosing a module (and speed) that is the correct size for your focus to process and perform with a high degree of perfection.

3. **Reinforcement** - Consistently and continuously repeating the select action(s) so that they become autonomous.

4. **Integration** – Reinforcing related modules by executing them either one after each other or together in order to form higher level modules.

5. **Escalation** - Selecting something new to practice that properly relates to your goals as you master previous modules.

We will now go on to look at these five processes one at a time...

Process #1 - Identification

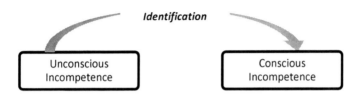

Figure 6: The Identification Process

The process of identification is actually very simple. As the name implies, the goal of this process is to identify what it is we are going to learn, or more accurately, going to practice.

How do we do this? We access our resources (consult a book, video, teacher, etc.) to find out **the difference(s) between how we are currently able to do something (or just plain unable) and how it could be done perfectly.**

This phase is about developing an awareness of what we need to practice and install in our minds.

Take particular note of the word 'perfectly'. Incomplete identification will lead you to only partial learning and the result will be substandard ability, so make sure you **identify all the factors that make up the perfect execution** of the module in question.

Essentially what we are doing here is setting the sights on what we will install into our brains.

If we aim at perfection and know what we are going to put in, it is far more likely that we will attain it.

Without identification, at best you will go through a complex cycle of trial and error, and at worst you will go down a dead end road and not even know what you are doing wrong (or right). Trying to do something without learning the proper way to do it is like 'reinventing the wheel.'

All you need to do in this process is **be** aware of what you need to learn, and how to do it perfectly. This process is one primarily based on asking two key questions...

1. What is the perfect way to do this module?
2. How does this differ from how I currently am able to do it?

Process #2 - Isolation

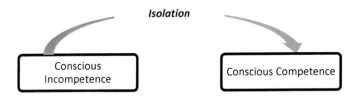

Figure 7: The Isolation Process

The Consistent Breaking Down of Material to a Rate That Your Conscious Mind Can Process.

This is perhaps the number one problem people have, a lack of isolation! Remember that we only have a limited conscious focus?

In identification we work out the exact perfect way that we would do something, but oftentimes we cannot work on it in one go (the amount of data is bigger than our conscious minds limit for focus).

We may know what we need to do (thanks to identification), but just knowing doesn't mean we will be able to do it instantly; remember that our ability is what is already in our mind (unconscious) and what we are able to focus on at any one time.

Given that when we learn something new it is not yet unconscious (it gets that way through practice), we need to make what we are learning small enough to fit in our conscious mind.

Have you ever been practicing and just felt that it wasn't getting you anywhere, and no matter how hard you tried you couldn't do it right? This is due to overwhelming your conscious mind with too much information.

The Symptoms of Overwhelm are the all too common situation of 'I just can't do it!' and the unproductive practice that results. The key emotion you will experience if you are overwhelmed is that of frustration, which serves as an instant warning sign that isolation is needed.

Also, a very high mistake rate (not being able to achieve the desired outcome for the majority of attempts) is also an indicator that you are overloading your mind with more data than your focus can process.

The key to isolation lies in reducing the amount of data you are focusing on, there are three key aspects that take up data in the performance of any module, namely **complexity, speed and perfection.**

Complexity	Speed	Perfection

Figure 9: The Three Factors that Increase the Load of Data

1. **Complexity** is simply how large a module you are focusing on. A higher level module has a higher complexity and higher volume of data than a lower level module and vice-versa.

2. **Speed** is how fast you execute the action that the module involves; doing something faster requires more data to be processed than doing something slow does.

3. **Perfection** is how close to the ideal way of performing the module you are. More perfection takes more data. The general measure of perfection is how often and how well you complete the objective of a module when attempting it.

Lowering any one of these three things will allow you to increase the other.

Ever notice you can do something more complex if you do it sloppily or slower? Or that you can do simple things quickly and perfectly without having to practice a lot? It's because at any one time in any module, these three factors make up your conscious data load, and they operate in a way that you can essentially trade off one for the other.

Either way will help you to get it down to the conscious minds capability of executing an amount of data that fits its capacity.

However, it is important to note that lowering perfection really should be your last option.

Ideally, your goal in learning should be the perfection of every individual module. As we learnt earlier, skills are a continual building of modules that together form higher levels (recall the pyramid-like structure of skills).

Without a 'strong foundation', so to speak, you will reach a stage where you will find great difficulties doing more advanced things or your performance in general will just seem sloppy.

Think of it like constructing a building. Having a weak foundation may hold the building up if it's only a single storey, but if there isn't enough bracing you will never be able to build the next storey up without it collapsing.

It is for this reason that it is better to seek a high-level of perfection from the get-go.

If you practice a complex module fast and with little perfection, practice will only reinforce that imperfection. However, if you slow down or lower the complexity while keeping perfection, over time as you practice you will be able to gradually increase complexity or bring the speed up.

That's not to say you can't improve by sacrificing perfection, but it is not the best way to learn, over time you will have to unlearn your bad habits and train in new ones if you consistently reinforce high amounts of imperfection.

While this doesn't sound very detrimental, it definitely can be. By having to 'unwire' incorrect actions and then having to practice the proper way of doing it, often you will end up doing twice the work in what is definitely a very inefficient strategy for learning.

Of course, there is the much rarer and opposite problem of **underwhelm,** which isn't too common but you should still be aware of. If you lower complexity and/or speed too much you will find it is not only too easy, but will experience the emotion of boredom. While this may not be as bad as trying to learn too much at once, it certainly is a signal that you could be learning more efficiently, so be sure to chunk up and/or speed up in this case.

Action Step(s):

Always practice something that is at the right level for your conscious mind to process.

Watch for the symptoms of overwhelm and underwhelm in order to tell you whether to focus on something smaller or bigger, and over time you will develop the intuition to know what you should be practicing before you even commence.

Always lower the data load by slowing it down and/or working on a lower level module, try to make sure you never unnecessarily sacrifice perfection.

Process #3 – Reinforcement

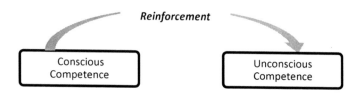

Figure 8: The Reinforcement Process

The process of repetition (or reinforcement) is what most people associate with practice.

It is simply the repetition of action(s) which in turn makes them become habitual and unconscious. Still, while seemingly simple there are a few things to consider when you engage in repetition.

Firstly, we tend to learn better when we are able to concentrate fully and free of distraction, worry and tension. This means it is a good idea to clear your mind before you practice. As out-there as it sounds, a few deep breathes will help.

Practicing with unnecessary strain will not only make for less reinforcement because your focus is impeded, but **may** also have the adverse effect of actually training in the discomfort – which is something we would definitely like to avoid.

That said, the **true secret** to perfecting the process of repetition lies in the amount you repeat, what you actually repeat and how consistent your repetition is.

Repeat Enough So It is Useful

It takes a certain amount of repetition before your brain 'gets the idea' that it should make it habitual (remember, anything done consistently and **continuously** becomes habitual).

If you are doing everything else right but just can't see improvement, you probably are not reinforcing enough before moving onto something else, so spend a longer period reinforcing the module by doing a larger number of repetitions.

Repeat the Right Thing

Not repeating a module correctly can be an absolutely enormous problem. Remember, repetition just makes whatever you are repeating habitual, it doesn't simply increase skill of its own accord.

Doing correct identification is one way to make sure you are reinforcing the correct action (or sequence of actions), but also make sure that you are consistent in and actually practice doing things perfectly, as slow as allows you to do it perfect (remember, the speed will come in time if you do it this way, if you don't the perfection will not come).

Also, be aware that when you are reinforcing a module, even though you are focusing on specific things, almost everything else you are doing is becoming reinforced if it is done consistently and continuously. You should pay attention to make sure that you are not unintentionally reinforcing things that could negatively affect you.

Be Consistent

Make sure you always reinforce the action by doing it the same way (ultimately, consistently perfect). If you have the option of learning multiple ways of achieving the exact same outcome it is preferable to train one in fully first. Remember, **consistently** and continuously.

If you juggle between two alternatives it will take longer for your brain to assimilate both as it doesn't have the required consistency to form a concrete habit as quickly. So, if there are two or more alternatives, get one down well to start, and later you can learn the others.

The same goes for any variations; some skills may require you to apply what you have learnt to different scenarios. Practice the variety of scenarios last, and work on a single scenario first (the most common or useful one is often the best choice).

Types of Repetition

As mentioned before, repetition does not always lead to skill. Certain ways of reinforcing will be more productive and produce better results than others.

Here is a simple guide...

Practice Made Perfect

Productive: Reinforcing proper actions and building effective neural pathways. By following the above guidelines, you will hopefully always be doing this kind.

Counter-Productive: Reinforcing the incorrect way of doing something. This is bad in many ways. Firstly, you are wasting time training in something that isn't right, and secondly, you are making it unconscious so you will need extra work to 'unlearn' it when you train in the proper way.

Unproductive: Changing what you practice too often and not reinforcing enough for what you are doing to become unconscious.

Process #4 – Integration

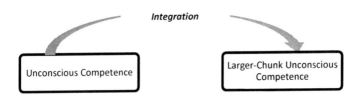

Figure 11: The Integration Process

By isolating and reinforcing, we put parts of a skill into our mind as just that, individual parts. An equally important part of practice is to integrate them by using our conscious focus to practice the various parts together and link the parts together into one to create a 'neural web'.

This gives us ability in a module that is of a higher level of abstraction. Think of integration as 'moving up' a level in the skill hierarchy.

You can integrate up to a relatively simple module (for example, joining together parts of a single dance move) or a complex one (joining together parts of a ten minute dance routine).

Integration is very important. Think of isolation as painting each piece of a puzzle individually. Now you need to connect them together to see the picture as a whole.

At any one time you can use your conscious focus to isolate and integrate. They can be done together, but you just won't be able to learn as big a piece in one go then. Either way, integration does happen.

There are two types of integration:

Concurrent

Here the parts of what you are learning all happen at the same time. For example, the various elements of correct posture while playing violin.

Figure 12: Concurrent Integration

In this case you may practice one part at a time, and then the whole. You may not need to learn one part at a time to be able to do whatever you are learning, but keep in mind you may need to focus specifically on individual modules if you want to perfect them to a high level.

By doing all processes and leaving out Integration, you will be able to do all individual parts fine, however you will be unable to do the actual activity as a whole. This is not a common problem, but one you may come across.

Sequential

This is just the joining together of parts that happen one after each other, like the aforementioned dance routine.

Figure 13: Sequential Integration

Process #5 – Escalation (Skill Increase)

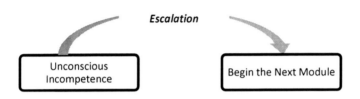

Figure 9: The Escalation Process

'Taking It to the Next Level'

Goal: Find your next level of possible ability.

Once we have practiced a module to the point where it is unconscious, (whether it is something entirely new or merely just an improvement) our conscious focus becomes freed and available for new learning.

In other words, we have 'improved' and are ready for our next thing to learn. After all, there is only so much we can reinforce what we already know.

We find ourselves back at the start, ready to identify a new inability that we can turn into ability.

Practice Made Perfect

This leads us to the end of the model, and consequently takes us back to the beginning — identifying a new module that will bring you closer to achieving your overall learning goals.

This process of returning back to the start is called escalation, and is very straightforward.

It brings us to the end of what is an infinite cycle, with each circle of it leading to an increase in talent, and a potential for infinite progress.

Perfect Practice: The Ultimate Skill

If you work hard at applying the principles in this book to anything you practice, you will develop them as an unconscious skill. That's right; it will get to the stage where when you pursue a skill you will get maximum results without even having to worry about the way you are practicing.

The legendary Greek philosopher Aristotle said it best,

'We are what we repeatedly do. Excellence then, is not an act, but a habit.'

That said, to achieve this unconscious competence of perfect practice you really do need to be consistently and continuously practicing using the principles in this book.

Continuousness is important, you need to keep applying these principles consciously, if you don't do it enough they will not become automatic.

Practice Made Perfect

Consistency is important, you need to apply the principles **whenever you practice**, so your mind gets the signal that this is the new way to practice **all the time**.

I understand that there is a lot of information in this section of book. So what I have tried to do is simplify it into a basic straightforward process that you can follow so it is easy for you to achieve this consistency.

By following this formula whenever you practice, you will find that eventually you will do it naturally and enjoy the benefits of maximum results in everything you do.

The 'Perfect Practice Method'

1. Choose the module you wish to install into your brain. Be aware of everything that relates to the perfect performance of it. (Identification)

2. Either Chunk Down or Slow Down until you find a module that you can do with a high degree of perfection. You are now focusing on the right amount of data. (Isolation)

3. Reinforce that module until it becomes unconscious. (Reinforcement)

4. Increase the Level of Speed and Continue to Practice until It is at the speed you desire (if you had previously slowed it down).

5. Repeat the above with modules on the same level of abstraction.

6. Practice doing all the modules together now as you join the ones that form a higher level module (Integration), until that becomes unconscious.

7. Find the next module you want to work on and repeat. (Escalation).

Part 3: Extra Things to Consider

Practice Schedules: The 'When' of Perfect Practice

There are a lot of questions that surround the timing of practice...

How much should I practice? How often should I practice? Should I practice for long amounts of time or short amounts? Should I take breaks in my practice? How often should I change the module that I am practicing?

Obviously at the end of the day the more practice the better, but there are benefits to be gained from proper spreading out of practice time, both for practice sessions as a whole, and the practice of specific modules.

A lot of this comes from the brain's process of taking time to properly assimilate what you have learnt, called maturation.

Maturation

Have you ever noticed sometimes while practicing you can't quite get something right, but overnight your ability increases and you can? Or as an extreme, after weeks of not practicing, it seems like you've gotten better?

You see the brain takes time to complete the learning process and arrange and store what you have taught it unconsciously (notice I said to 'complete' the learning process, you can of course learn something unconsciously in one session) and this process is called **maturation** by scientists.

Sometimes an adequate amount of maturation is needed before we are to become competent in something, or to solidify the lower modules of a skill that form the base of learning more complicated modules. Both short and long periods of maturation tend to have an effect.

Understand though that maturation comes as the result of practice, you do not just get better by doing nothing – it is the result of the practice that you have already done.

That said, this doesn't mean we should only practice a little and then expect maturation do the rest, it just doesn't work that way.

Ideally we want to do as much practice as possible, but we can use this knowledge of maturation to help us better organise how we practice.

The most important thing we can learn from this is that, due to maturation, **a large amount of smaller practice sessions will produce greater results than a few large ones**.

The reason behind this is that smaller practice sessions with breaks between allows time for maturation and thus results in more progress.

The same principle applies on a micro level within our own practice sessions, rather than focusing on one module for several hours at a time, it is better to split up what we learn and cycle through modules to give the one we have just practiced a little time to mature. Often you will find that if you work on something else for a little bit and then return to a previous module, you will find it considerably easier.

Also, if there is something that you have been practicing a lot (and with perfect practice) and you still can't do it or do it well, your time is better spent on something else as what you've been practicing likely just needs some time to mature.

It's not very common to get 'plateaus' when you are doing perfect practice, but if you do, it is almost always because you just need to give what you have learnt time to mature. Remember, **if you are doing perfect practice, it is impossible for you not to improve.** Sometimes you just need to give your brain time to assimilate what it has learnt.

Also, you may occasionally experience days when your performance is sub-par, don't let this get to you, this phenomena of 'bad days and good days' is just the result of maturation and rest assured that as long as you are practicing right, the trend in your skill level will be considerably upwards in the long term.

Reactivation

There is another phenomenon that I call 'reactivation'.

Have you ever noticed that after you haven't done something in a while it's like your skill for it has disappeared, only to find that you return to your old level of skill with just a little practice?

This is simply because your old neural pathways haven't been used in a while, but by accessing them again you re-link them up to your neural network and they come back quite quickly. Think of it like 'dusting off the cobwebs' of your neural connections.

So don't worry if you've learnt something, taken a break and suddenly it seems like your skill has disappeared. The simple process of trying to do what you used to be able to do will bring back the skill even from a long time ago, as long as you remind yourself how to do it right (a little identification may be required).

Whether you haven't practiced for a day, a month or a year, your brain always requires some amount of reactivation before you are back in your usual form.

It is for this reason that **warm-ups** can be so effective, especially in more complex skills. A lot of people warm up to help condition their muscles so they don't suffer from repetitive strain injuries, but warm-ups serve a dual purpose in that they also help reactivate your neural pathways.

Warm-ups tend to be general and lower-level module based and as such help the performance of the skill as a whole reactivate.

You will notice that if you don't warm up and just go straight to doing more complex modules it will take longer for you to reactivate (ie. get back to your average level of skill) than it would if you were to spend time warming up by working on or just simply performing some lower level modules.

Practice Made Perfect

> ***Action Step:*** At the start of each practice session, perform a set of general and lower-level, module-based exercises in order to help you reactivate faster.

Mental Practice

Ironically, the human mind cannot tell the difference between a real and an imagined experience – this is a concept used widely by self-help authors but the same applies for the way that the mind learns skills as well.

The same building of neural pathways occurs by imagining practice as it does by actually doing practice. Mental practice is almost, if not as effective, as real practice.

In fact most practices include some imagined, unrealistic or simulated component as the environments and situations in which you practice in are rarely exactly the same as those which you will ultimately perform the skill in.

The mind has the good knowledge to know when to apply in the real world things that were simulated or imagined.

It's not that we should necessarily worry about doing mental practice instead of real practice, as both give similar results, but rather, **we should include mental components in our real practice when they are not present in our practice situation**.

For example, anytime you are training a skill that involves anything outside of you that affects you or you need to react to, it is highly beneficial to imagine that as part of your practice. Imagine it happening, and then practice responding to it, as opposed to just practicing the response by itself all the time.

Of course, this doesn't mean that you can't or shouldn't do practice that is **entirely** mental. There are times when it is your only option, for example if you are injured, when it is physically impossible to practice for a long time without becoming physically exhausted, or at times when you just plain don't have the materials with you that you require to do regular practice.

Beyond Practice: Perfect Performance

At the end of the day most skills we learn will have some sort of practical application, which requires the 'performance' of the skill in question in real time and in the real world (that is, outside of your practice space).

Where practice is the preparation, performance is the tangible purposeful execution of what you have learned to actually achieve the goal of the skill-set (or part of the skill-set) that you have learnt.

Seeming we have worked so hard to practice so well to gain this skill, it would be wise to ask 'is there anything else we can think of that will help our performance of it?' The answer to this question is a resounding yes. There are a few things I will discuss and they stem from understanding the distinction between practice and performance.

Practice is using your conscious focus to improve, but using our conscious focus (mind) isn't really something that should not take place during 'performance'.

Performance is the actual doing of what you have learnt **unconsciously.** You really need a deeply engrained unconscious competence for real world performance, because outside factors need to be taken into consideration.

You see, in practice, you can control a lot, but in performance there is often an added element of **stress** – that is People watching, emotional duress of competition, performance anxiety, thoughts of failure, and so forth.

*Stress can be any o*utside influence that either,

        a. Affects our own consciousness or

        b. We need to process and react to.

All performance involves some form of 'stress'. That is, something that affects us that is not really there when we practice, and as such detracts from overall skill. Have you ever noticed that when the crunch time comes your skill just seems to go down and you choke? That's due to stress.

It's true that we can't control stressing factors, but we can decrease the amount of effect they have on our skill level during performance.

The solution is simple. The more deeply unconsciously competent we are, the more **resilient we are to stress** and thus likely to perform properly (that is, achieve the desired goal of our skill).

Remember how through conscious focus we can change what is habitual? It is because of this outside stress that our consciousness falters and we literally 'get in our own way' of what we have already trained in, what we already know how to do and probably have done right many times.

In traditional eastern martial arts there is a concept of 'No-Mindedness', which is a mental state when a performer isn't occupied or fixated by thought or emotion, which allows their conscious mind to be open to respond better to what is coming at them, not to mention preventing it from getting in their own way.

The aforementioned leads us to two **very important and practical** points...

We should train ourselves in practice to a level of unconscious competence where performance requires no conscious competence **whatsoever.** In fact, it is advantageous to keep reinforcing past the point of unconscious competence so your skill is so deeply engrained that it becomes more resilient to stress.

AND

We should try not to consciously indulge in any thoughts or extra focus when we perform (remember, you should know how to do it already from practice) and rather just let our consciousness watch ourselves do the skill.

You may also want to imagine the stresses of performance in your normal practice as a mental component (or better yet, do something in reality to simulate the stress, though this is often not possible). This will help improve your execution for when the actual performance situation comes along.

Developing the Habit of Practice

At the end of the day, we should be trying to get ourselves to consistently do more practice, because more practice ultimately means more skill. Doing practice and doing a lot of it is a matter of **habit** more than anything else, motivation is useless unless it can help you build that habit.

If you can adequately and strongly build the habit of practicing for one, two or even five hours daily it will become automatic and you will find it will be **harder to not practice**.

The same concept that underlies perfect practice also underlies doing a lot of regular practice,

> *'Anything that you do consistently and*
> *continuously becomes habitual.'*

The catch is before you can enjoy this however is you first need to consciously build the habit through repetition, and then it will become unconscious as long as it is executed **consistently and continually.**

Practice Made Perfect

You will need to practice **every day, for the desired amount.** The key is consistency; you will need to reinforce the habit every day for at least a few weeks for it to become a strong habit.

The question is, how do we get ourselves to do that?

To build a habit, we need the discipline to take action consistently, and that can only come from motivation.

Think of motivation and action that follows as the original 'sparks' that light a fire which continues to burn, or rekindle a fire to keep it burning if somehow we fall out of habit.

Initially we have a habit of doing little to no practice, and this has been deeply unconsciously engrained through years of not practicing or not practicing enough.

Due to the fact that this habit is so deeply engrained, we really need some sort of momentum to get us to act and break it. This momentum is motivation.

Practice Made Perfect

Once we have enough motivation, we drive ourselves to consistent action and eventually an unconscious habit is formed. Similar to learning a module, once we have engrained a habit unconsciously, this now leaves our conscious mind open to build a new habit of doing even more practice.

Of course, this whole process begins with motivation. So how do we get the motivation to act? The remaining part of this part of the book will look at some things that help build and maintain motivation.

Inspiration

Being properly inspired is a key driver for the motivation that will enable you to take the required action and build the habit of practicing regularly.

Inspiration is mainly a matter of getting clear **why** you are learning the skill, and opening your eyes to the benefits of doing so. Being inspired is nothing more than your perception of possessing your skill as having a great amount of value to you.

Simply put, to be properly motivated, we need to have greater perception from the good outcomes that will arise from our practice than we do for our energy exerted practicing.

People tend to be more motivated if they have a vision that excites them. This vision is simply the sum total of everything that acquiring the skill will give them.

So ask yourself,

Practice Made Perfect

'What will attaining my goals in this skill enable me to do, and what else will it give me?

Remember it's the 'perceived value' (also known as 'utility') that causes motivation. That is, how much you perceive the skill to have value to you. By becoming clear and constantly diverting your focus onto why you want to acquire the skill, you will notice an increase in motivation.

A skill's utility is subjective, not objective, and because of this you can begin to increase it and thus increase your motivation.

Question yourself, 'Why do I want to this?', true motivation to do something comes from the deep desire when a person really wants to do an activity, not feels that they 'have to' for no particular reason.

As the saying goes, "You can put a gun to a person's head to make them act, but they'll stop as soon as you take away the gun."

Action Step: *Increasing Utility*

Firstly, have a vision of where you are ultimately headed that excites you.

Write down the specific reasons why you want to get learn or master your skill to the level you aspire to and focus on it regularly. Try to come up with and write down as many reasons as possible.

This list can and should include any mental, physical or emotional benefits from practicing and mastering your chosen skill.

Make sure that these reasons make you feel that you **want** to do it, not that you **have to.**

The Peak Practice Experience (Flow)

We've talked a lot about making more progress quicker, but what about actually enjoying the act of practice? It makes perfect sense that the more you enjoy your practice, the more you will practice, and as a result the better you will get.

This is far from a motivational waste of time or an airy-fairy notion of idealism, the simple fact is one part of the mastery equation is motivation, and motivation itself is largely determined by your experience practicing.

When I mention 'Peak Experience' however, I mean a lot more than simply 'having fun', what I'm talking about is the concept of 'Flow', which is more commonly referred to as 'being in the zone'.

Psychologist *Mihály Csíkszentmihályi* has dedicated almost an entire career to the study of Flow and Peak Experience, so for anyone looking to find out more I recommend you read his works, in particular 'Flow: The Psychology of Optimal Experience"

Being in flow is a fantastic experience and attaining this state should be your goal whenever you are practicing; it is very similar to the concept of 'No-Mind' that was discussed regarding performance.

Finding the 'Sweet Spot'

Mihály mentions in his work that a big part of getting into this flow state is not only having goals, but having them of the right size and challenge.

This is similar to the concept of 'Isolation', where we would take things that we had to learn and break them down into chunks that our conscious minds were able to process.

A very similar thing happens when it comes to goals, in that if an immediate goal is too hard to achieve, you will be overwhelmed, and if it far too easy, you will be underwhelmed.

Practice Made Perfect

This is an important key to unlocking your motivation.

When you find the 'sweet spot' in isolation, it's more or less one of the major pieces of the puzzle to solving 'practice effectiveness'.

When you find out how to find it in setting learning goals as a whole, it will prove to be one of the major pieces of the puzzle in getting 'motivation' solved.

Action Step: Make sure what you hope to achieve in one practice session is big enough to inspire and challenge you, yet small enough to achieve.

Purpose-Based Practice vs. Time-Based Practice

Most, if not all people, tend to structure their practice sessions around time, as in, "I will practice X for 2 hours every day" or "I'll practice from when I wake up till when I have to go to work."

This method is great in the sense that we all need that sense of consistency (and continuity) to build a habit, however there is one flaw in this approach.

It is the mind's unconscious tendency to take the path of least effort when you present it with a goal.

Think about it, have you ever put aside half an hour for practice and found that you wasted it on nothing in particular, and your mind seemingly just drifted away from you?

Of course it did, you told yourself that you were going to practice for half an hour, and unconsciously your mind decided, via taking the path of least effort, that it was going to do as little as it could to make you pass those thirty minutes.

We can overcome this problem by making the purpose of your practice primarily purpose and goal-oriented.

It is of course still important to do a lot of practice time-wise, but that should be of secondary importance.

Practice Made Perfect

Often you will find, once you get absorbed in flow and achieving your goal, you will spend more time than you would have otherwise set for yourself to practice. You may pass two hours effortlessly, when normally you would have to force yourself to do just half an hour.

One of the characteristics of a flow experience is that one tends to lose their sense of time, so naturally if you are constantly focusing on and worrying about time, you are naturally going to resist flow, enjoy yourself less, and improve less.

Not only will primarily purpose driven practice give you a better experience (via flow), it will also give you better results, **both of which will increase your motivation!**

Action Step: _Setting Purpose and Time_

Before you begin to practice, identify specifically the goal of what you are aiming to achieve in **that particular session** (what module or modules you hope to learn and perfect) **and** the minimum time you are allocating for that practice session.

By sticking to both, you will have a more productive and enjoyable practice session. Just be sure that the time limit is secondary, what is truly important is the purpose.

Belief in Success

One of the most important things that can affect a person's motivation and persistence is how much they actually believe they will be able to achieve their goals.

It's **very** easy to give up if you think all of your work is going to waste, or that your efforts may be amounting to absolutely nothing. Conversely, it is very hard to give up if you are absolutely sure that mastering your skill to the level that you desire is easily within your grasp.

As the earlier chapters on natural talent and the human mind explained, there really are very little limits that you have.

Knowing that success is possible is one thing, but after reading this book and following it, you will go one step further, you will not only know that success is not only possible, but that it is **inevitable** as long as you practice and practice properly.

Action Step:

If you ever find yourself doubting that you can reach your desired level of skill in your chosen skill-set, be sure to *reassure yourself* by rereading Part I of this book and understanding that as long as you practice properly, you will improve.

Success Loops

You may have heard the saying **'Success Causes Success'.** This is something that is absolutely true. The accomplishment of tangible results causes a burst of motivation, which in turn produces even more results. This is what is known as a 'success loop'.

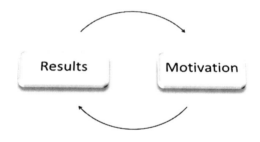

Figure 15: The Success Loop

Likewise, a lack of results over a period of time will result in a decrease of motivation as one begins to question the worth of their effort, spiralling into giving up.

Practice Made Perfect

It is the **natural inclination** of the human mind to prefer immediate gratification over long term results. This is generally a negative trait but why not use it to your advantage?

In order to do this, you should keep things you are learning as fresh and as new as you possibly can, this helps combat boredom.

Action Step:

While sometimes it is unavoidable that certain parts of a skill take extended periods of practice before they give tangible results, whenever you feel the onset of boredom or a lull in motivation, switch to practicing something that will give you immediate results.

This will boost your motivation and allow you to see out the harder and longer periods of learning. Variety in your practice, in general, is a good way to go about this.

Final Words

There we go, in less than a hundred pages we have literally decoded and provided you a complete guide for becoming 'talented'.

However, this is only the beginning; the rest is now up to you.

When all is said and done, there is no magic pill that will suddenly make you a virtuoso of your chosen skill; you still need to put in the work.

That said, you will now progress much quicker and easier by following this guide. Be sure to refer back to it as much as is necessary as you practice.

In closing, I wish you all the best on your path, whatever it may be and only hope that this book will bring you much closer to attaining your goals.

Faithfully,

Roberto Moretti

Lightning Source UK Ltd.
Milton Keynes UK
11 September 2009

143579UK00001B/27/P